AF480111

A

GUIDE

TO

GOOD

PARENTING

A GUIDE TO GOOD PARENTING

Ursula Davis

Davis Book Publishing
Summerville, South Carolina

A GUIDE TO GOOD PARENTING

Published by
Davis Book Publishing
Summerville, South Carolina
ursulakershaw@gmail.com

Ursula Davis, Publisher / Editorial Director
Yvonne Rose/QualityPress.info, Book Packager

Copyright © 2024 by Ursula Davis
Hardcover ISBN: 979-8-8692-3447-6
Ebook ISBN: 979-8-8692-3448-3
Library of Congress Control Number: 2024905017

Dedication

I would like to dedicate this book to my amazing children, Tracy, Tierra, Jamal, Jarvis, and Jarrett.

Acknowledgments

I sat in my room one night thinking to myself, *it is so hard being a young parent, there has to be a way I can help someone with parenting, giving some tips that I learned along the way.* I had a lot of people around me to give me great parenting advice, yet I did not have a role model to follow. The old saying "it takes a village to raise a child" is true to a certain extent.

I want to thank the ladies in parenting class, my family, my best friends, my next-door neighbor who would babysit from time to time, and my church family (The Village)

Table of Contents

A Guide to Good Parenting

Preface

As a teenage mom, confused and illiterate about parenting. I fought with the struggle of how to do proper parenting and wondered where I should start. Wishing I had some type of guide to help me with parenting, I had a hard time putting things in place other than the obvious feeding and changing diapers, while thinking to myself, *what's next?*

This is my guide written especially for you as you embark upon your journey of motherhood.

Introduction

Because my childhood and my upbringing were not the best because of terrible living conditions and sometimes being in situations that would put me in danger of predators, I was overprotective. I did what I knew, and I made a lot of mistakes that strengthened my knowledge of parenting. This made me want to do better as a parent. So, I figured I would just put what I learned in writing, hoping it would help someone.

The truth is every parent wants to be the best parent they can be and bringing a child into this world you have one shot at getting it right; you can't get a do-over with that child. So, I will do the best I can with what I know. With God, being the head of my life, I taught my children spiritual grounds and to be kind to others. I believe there's no right or wrong way to be a parent, but we can learn from each other. I pray for your great success with the tips I have shared.

SWEET DREAMS

Sweet Dreams

As parents, we all want the best for our children. We want them to grow up happy, healthy, and well-adjusted. One crucial aspect of their well-being is ensuring they get the sweet dreams they deserve.

Sleep plays a vital role in a child's development. During sleep, their bodies heal, their brains process information, and their emotions stabilize. When children get enough restful sleep, they are more focused, have better memory retention, and are generally happier throughout the day.

So, how can we, as parents, ensure that our children have sweet dreams and get the sleep they need? Here are some valuable tips to guide you on this journey:

Establish a Consistent Bedtime Routine: Children thrive on routine and predictability.

Create a Soothing Bedtime Routine that includes activities like reading a bedtime story, taking a warm bath, or listening to calming music. This routine will signal to your child that it's time to wind down and prepare for sleep.

Create a Calm and Comfortable Sleep Environment: A peaceful sleep environment is essential for promoting sweet dreams. Make sure your child's bedroom is quiet, dark, and at a comfortable temperature.

Provide a Cozy and Supportive Mattress, soft bedding, and their favorite stuffed animal or blanket for added comfort.

Limit Screen Time Before Bed: The blue light emitted by electronic devices can interfere with your child's sleep patterns. Establish a screen-free zone at least an hour before bedtime. Encourage quiet activities like reading, drawing, or gentle stretching instead.

Encourage Physical Activity: Regular exercise can greatly contribute to better sleep. Encourage your child to engage in physical activities during the day, such as playing outside, riding a bike, or participating in organized sports. However, ensure that they finish any vigorous exercise at least a few hours before bedtime, as it can be stimulating.

Avoid Stimulating Foods and Drinks: Certain foods and drinks can disrupt sleep patterns, leading to restless nights. Limit your child's consumption of caffeine-containing beverages like soda or energy drinks. Opt for healthier alternatives like herbal tea or warm milk before bed. Additionally, avoid sugary snacks or heavy meals close to bedtime, as they can cause discomfort and indigestion.

Be Attentive to Sleep Safety: Create a safe sleep environment for your child. Ensure their crib or bed meets current safety standards, and never place any objects or loose bedding that might pose a suffocation risk. Keep your child's sleep area free from hazards and ensure they are dressed appropriately for the temperature.

Address Nighttime Fears: Children often experience fears or anxieties that can disrupt their sleep. Take the time to listen to their concerns and reassure them. Consider using a night light or providing a comforting object to help alleviate any fears they may have.

Monitor and Adjust Sleep Schedules: Keep track of your child's sleep patterns and adjust their bedtime if necessary. Ensure they are getting the recommended amount of sleep for their age group. Remember, every child is different, and their sleep needs may vary.

In Conclusion: By implementing these practices, you can create a nurturing environment that promotes sweet dreams for your child.

So, dear parents, let's embark on this journey together and guide our children towards the sweet dreams they deserve.

Remember, good parenting involves prioritizing your child's sleep and ensuring they have the best possible chance for a restful night.

BUILDING A FOUNDATION OF LOVE

Building a Foundation of Love

As parents, we all want our children to grow up feeling loved and secure. We want them to have sweet dreams and wake up each day knowing they are cherished. But how do we build this foundation of love that will support them throughout their lives?

The answer lies in the language of love itself. Love is not just a feeling; it is a verb, an action that we can actively cultivate and nurture in our parenting journey. It starts with the small, everyday gestures that show our children they are loved and valued.

One of the most important ways to build a foundation of love is through unconditional acceptance. Our children need to know that they are loved for who they are, not for what they achieve or how they behave. When we offer them our unwavering love, regardless of their mistakes or shortcomings, we create a safe space where they can truly be themselves.

Another vital aspect of building a foundation of love is the power of presence. In our busy lives, it's easy to get caught up in the never-ending to-do lists and distractions. But our children need our undivided attention and presence. By giving them our time and being fully present when we interact with them, we communicate that they are important and that we genuinely care about them.

Communication is another key ingredient in building a foundation of love. We must strive to create an open and honest dialogue with our children, where they feel comfortable expressing their thoughts and feelings. This means actively listening to them without judgment, validating their emotions, and offering guidance and support when needed.

Consistency and reliability are also crucial in nurturing a foundation of love. Children thrive on routine and predictability. When they know they can rely on us to be there for them, to keep our promises, and to provide a stable environment, they feel secure and loved.

Physical affection is a language of love that speaks volumes. Hugs, kisses, and gentle touches are not only comforting, but they also strengthen the bond between parent and child. By regularly expressing our love through physical touch, we create a sense of warmth and security that our children will carry with them throughout their lives.

Lastly, leading by example is fundamental in building a foundation of love. Children learn by observing and imitating their parents' behavior. By modeling love, kindness, empathy, and respect in our everyday actions, we teach them how to navigate relationships and build healthy connections with others.

Building a foundation of love is an ongoing process that requires time, patience, and dedication. It may not always be easy, and we may stumble along the way, but by consistently practicing these principles, we will create a nurturing environment where our children can thrive.

In conclusion, building a foundation of love is about actively showing our children that they are cherished, accepted, and valued. It is about being present, communicating openly, offering consistency and reliability, expressing physical affection, and leading by example.

Remember: By incorporating these practices into our parenting journey, we lay the groundwork for our children to have sweet dreams and a lifetime filled with love.

CREATING A SAFE AND SECURE ENVIRONMENT

Creating a Safe and Secure Environment

In this chapter, we will explore various ways in which we can create a safe and secure environment for our little ones. First and foremost, it is essential to establish clear boundaries and rules within our homes.

As parents, one of our most important roles is to create an environment that is safe and secure for our children. This not only ensures their physical well-being but also contributes to their emotional and psychological development.

Children thrive when they know what is expected of them and what behavior is acceptable. Setting consistent and age-appropriate guidelines helps them feel secure and understand the consequences of their actions.

By creating a structure and routine, we provide a sense of stability that is crucial for their overall well-being. Additionally, ensuring the physical safety of our children is paramount.

We must carefully childproof our homes, removing any potential hazards or dangers that could harm them. This includes securing cabinets and drawers, covering electrical outlets, and installing safety gates to prevent falls downstairs. Regularly inspecting toys for any loose parts or broken pieces is also crucial to avoid accidents. By taking these precautions, we can significantly reduce the risk of accidents and injuries.

Emotional safety is equally important in creating a secure environment for our children. We must be attentive to their feelings and provide a supportive and nurturing atmosphere where they feel comfortable expressing themselves. Listening actively and validating their emotions helps them develop a sense of trust and security. Creating open lines of communication allows them to seek guidance when needed and strengthens the bond between parent and child.

Another vital aspect of creating a safe environment is fostering positive relationships within the family. Encouraging healthy interactions and resolving conflicts peacefully teaches children how to navigate relationships and builds their social skills. By modeling empathy, kindness, and respect, we provide them with a secure foundation from which they can grow and develop strong relationships with others.

In today's digital age, it is crucial to address internet safety as well. Teaching children about online risks, setting limits on screen time, and monitoring their online activities are essential for their protection. Educating ourselves about internet safety and staying informed about the latest trends and threats allows us to guide and protect our children effectively.

Lastly, creating a safe and secure environment means instilling a sense of self-confidence and independence in our children. Encouraging them to take risks, make decisions, and learn from their mistakes helps them develop resilience and self-reliance. By allowing them age-appropriate freedoms and responsibilities, we empower them to navigate the world with confidence while knowing they have a safe haven to return to.

In conclusion, creating a safe and secure environment for our children is a fundamental aspect of parenting. By setting clear boundaries, ensuring physical safety, fostering emotional well-being, promoting positive relationships, addressing internet safety, and nurturing independence, we provide our children with the tools they need to thrive.

Remember, a safe and secure environment lays the foundation for their overall development and allows them to grow into happy, confident, and resilient individuals.

SETTING LIMITS AND MAINTAINING DISCIPLINE

Setting Limits and Maintaining Discipline

In this chapter, we will explore effective strategies for establishing limits and maintaining discipline in a way that fosters a loving and respectful relationship with our children.

In the journey of parenting, one of the most crucial aspects is setting limits and maintaining discipline for our children. It is through these boundaries that we guide them toward responsible behavior and help them develop self-control. However, this task can be challenging, as it requires consistency, patience, and understanding.

First and foremost, it is essential to recognize that setting limits is not about restricting our children or asserting control over them. Instead, it is about providing them with a safe and structured environment where they can thrive. By setting clear boundaries, we create a sense of security and predictability that allows our children to feel confident and explore the world around them.

To effectively establish limits, it is crucial to be consistent in our expectations. Children thrive on routine and consistency, as it helps them understand what is expected of them. When we set limits, we must ensure that they are reasonable and age-appropriate. By considering our child's developmental stage, we can tailor our expectations to their abilities, making it easier for them to succeed.

Another key aspect of setting limits is communicating them clearly to our children. Instead of simply stating what they cannot do, we should also explain why certain boundaries are in place. By providing them with logical explanations, we help them understand the importance of these limits and encourage their cooperation. It is important to remember that children are more likely to follow rules when they understand the reasoning behind them.

While setting limits is crucial, maintaining discipline is equally important. Discipline should never be about punishment or control but rather about teaching our children how to make responsible choices. When disciplinary action is necessary, it should be done in a calm and loving manner. By using positive reinforcement and constructive criticism, we can guide our children toward better behavior while preserving their self-esteem. It is essential to remember that discipline should always be rooted in empathy and understanding.

When our children make mistakes, it is an opportunity for growth and learning. Instead of reacting with anger or frustration, we should approach these situations with empathy and a willingness to teach. By focusing on problem-solving and teaching alternative behaviors, we can help our children develop the skills they need to make better choices in the future.

Maintaining discipline also requires us to lead by example. Our actions speak louder than words, and our children learn more from what we do than what we say. It is important to model the behavior we want to see in our children, demonstrating respect, kindness, and self-control. By embodying these qualities, we create a positive environment that encourages our children to follow suit.

Lastly, it is crucial to remember that setting limits and maintaining discipline is an ongoing process. As our children grow and develop, our strategies may need to adapt accordingly. It is important to stay open-minded and flexible, willing to reassess our approach and make necessary adjustments. Parenting is a continuous learning experience, and by being responsive to our children's changing needs, we can create a nurturing environment where they can flourish.

In conclusion, setting limits and maintaining discipline is a fundamental aspect of parenting. By providing our children with clear boundaries, communicating expectations, and maintaining consistency, we help them develop self-control and responsible behavior. It is through empathy, understanding, and positive reinforcement that we guide our children towards making better choices.

Remember, parenting is a journey, and by embracing the challenges, we can raise happy, confident, and well-disciplined children.

CHAPTER 5

HELPING CHILDREN DEVELOP SELF-CONTROL

Helping Children Develop Self-Control

In this chapter, we will explore the importance of nurturing self-control in children and how it can positively impact their development. Self-control, often referred to as the ability to regulate one's own behavior, is an essential life skill that lays the foundation for future success.

As parents, it is our responsibility to guide our children toward developing self-control in a loving and supportive manner. One of the key aspects of helping children develop self-control is setting consistent and clear boundaries.

By establishing age-appropriate rules and expectations, we provide a structure that enables children to understand what acceptable behavior is. These boundaries should be communicated calmly and consistently and reinforced with appropriate consequences when necessary.

It is crucial to remember that children learn best through observation and imitation. As parents, we serve as role models for our children's behavior. Therefore, it is important to demonstrate self-control in our own actions and reactions. By remaining calm and composed in challenging situations, we teach our children the value of self-regulation.

Another effective strategy for fostering self-control is providing children with opportunities to make choices and solve problems independently. Encouraging them to think critically and consider the consequences of their actions helps them develop impulse control and decision-making skills. By allowing children to experience the natural outcomes of their choices, we empower them to take responsibility for their behavior.

Teaching children emotional intelligence is also essential in their journey towards self-control. Emotions play a significant role in behavior, and children need to learn how to identify and manage their feelings appropriately. By helping them recognize and express their emotions in a healthy manner, we equip them with the tools to regulate their behavior effectively.

Patience is a virtue, especially when it comes to helping children develop self-control. It is important to remember that self-control is a gradual process that takes time and practice. Instead of expecting instant results, we should celebrate small victories and offer praise and encouragement along the way. By acknowledging and reinforcing their efforts, we motivate children to continue working towards self-control.

Additionally, it is crucial to create a supportive environment that promotes self-control. By providing a consistent routine, adequate sleep, and a healthy diet, we can help children maintain physical and emotional well-being, which directly affects their ability to regulate their behavior.

Furthermore, offering alternative outlets for stress and frustration, such as engaging in physical activities or practicing mindfulness, can provide children with healthy coping mechanisms.

In conclusion, helping children develop self-control is an essential aspect of parenting. By setting clear boundaries, being positive role models, encouraging independent decision-making, teaching emotional intelligence, and fostering patience, we can assist our children in developing this valuable life skill.

Remember, with our support and guidance, they will be well-equipped to navigate challenges and make thoughtful choices that will positively impact their lives.

PROMOTING HEALTHY EATING HABITS

Promoting Healthy Eating Habits

In this chapter, we will explore effective strategies for promoting healthy eating habits in our little ones.

As parents, we play a vital role in shaping our children's eating habits. The choices we make and the examples we set can have a lasting impact on their overall health and well-being.

One of the first steps in promoting healthy eating habits is to provide a variety of nutritious foods. Introducing a wide range of fruits, vegetables, whole grains, lean proteins, and dairy products can help create a well-rounded diet for our children. By offering a diverse selection of foods, we can expose them to different flavors and textures, thus expanding their palates and encouraging them to make healthier choices.

Another important aspect of promoting healthy eating habits is to establish regular meal and snack times. Having a structured eating schedule helps children develop a sense of routine and control over their hunger cues. Encouraging them to eat at the table, away from distractions like television or mobile devices, can also foster a mindful eating experience. This way, they can focus on their food and recognize their body's signals of fullness.

It is crucial to be mindful of our own eating habits as well. As parents, we are our children's role models, and they often imitate what they see us do. By demonstrating healthy eating behaviors ourselves, such as choosing nutritious snacks and enjoying balanced meals, we can inspire our children to follow suit. It is important to remember that our words and actions carry great influence, so let's make conscious choices that promote healthy eating.

Incorporating children into the meal planning and preparation process can be an enjoyable and educational way to encourage healthy eating. By involving them in grocery shopping, meal preparation, and even gardening, we can instill a sense of ownership and curiosity about the foods they consume. This hands-on approach can help them develop a positive relationship with food, as they witness the effort and care that goes into preparing wholesome meals.

Alongside meal planning and preparation, it is important to limit the availability of sugary snacks and beverages in our homes. While occasional treats are acceptable, creating a balanced and nutritious environment can help our children make healthier choices. Stocking our pantries with wholesome snacks like fruits, nuts, and yogurt can provide them with nutritious alternatives when cravings strike.

Promoting healthy eating habits also involves fostering a positive and supportive atmosphere around food. Instead of focusing on restrictions or labeling certain foods as "good" or "bad," let's encourage our children to listen to their bodies and make mindful choices. Teaching them about the importance of moderation and balance can empower them to make informed decisions about their own nutrition.

Lastly, it is essential to remember that promoting healthy eating habits is a journey, not a destination. As children grow and develop, their tastes and preferences may change. It is important to remain patient and adaptable, continuing to offer a variety of nutritious foods and encouraging them to explore new flavors. By establishing a foundation of healthy eating habits early on, we can set our children on a path towards a lifetime of nourishment and well-being.

In conclusion, by providing a diverse range of nutritious foods, establishing regular meal and snack times, setting a positive example, involving our children in meal planning and preparation, limiting sugary snacks, and fostering a supportive food environment, we can create a foundation for lifelong health and well-being.

Remember. Let's embrace this opportunity to nourish our children's bodies and minds through the power of healthy eating habits.

ENCOURAGING GOOD COMMUNICATION

Encouraging Good Communication

In the realm of parenting, communication plays a pivotal role in fostering a healthy and nurturing relationship with our children. It is through effective communication that we can truly understand the needs, desires, and concerns of our little ones. As parents, it is our responsibility to create an environment that encourages open and honest dialogue, enhancing the bond we share with our children.

Communication is a two-way street, and it is important to remember that it involves not only speaking but also listening. When we actively listen to our children, we validate their feelings and lct them know that their thoughts and opinions matter. By giving them our undivided attention, we create a safe space for them to share their triumphs, fears, and dreams.

One of the most powerful tools we have as parents is empathy. By putting ourselves in our children's shoes, we can better understand their perspective and respond with compassion and understanding. When our children feel heard and validated, they are more likely to open up and share their thoughts and feelings with us.

To encourage good communication, we must create an atmosphere of trust and respect. By fostering a sense of trust, our children will feel comfortable sharing even their most vulnerable thoughts and emotions. We can build this trust by being reliable, keeping our promises, and honoring their confidentiality. By modeling respectful behavior, we teach our children how to communicate with kindness and consideration.

In today's fast-paced world, it is easy to get caught up in the whirlwind of daily activities. However, it is crucial to prioritize quality time with our children. By setting aside dedicated moments to connect and engage in meaningful conversations, we show our children that they are a priority in our lives. This uninterrupted time allows us to truly listen and respond with intention, strengthening our bond and creating a foundation for open communication.

As parents, we must also be mindful of our own communication habits. Our children are always watching and learning from us. By being mindful of our tone, body language, and choice of words, we can model effective communication skills. It is important to remember that our actions speak louder than our words, and our children are more likely to emulate behavior that they witness firsthand.

Technology has become an integral part of our lives, and while it has its benefits, it can also hinder good communication. It is essential to set boundaries around screen time and create tech-free zones where we can focus on connecting with our children without distractions. By limiting our own screen time and being fully present when engaging with our children, we demonstrate the importance of face-to-face communication.

In conclusion, encouraging good communication with our children is a fundamental aspect of parenting. By actively listening, empathizing, creating trust, spending quality time, modeling respectful behavior, and minimizing distractions, we can foster an environment that promotes open and honest dialogue.

Remember, through effective communication, we deepen our connection with our children, strengthen their self-confidence, and create a foundation for a lifetime of healthy relationships.

TEACHING RESPECT AND RESPONSIBILITY

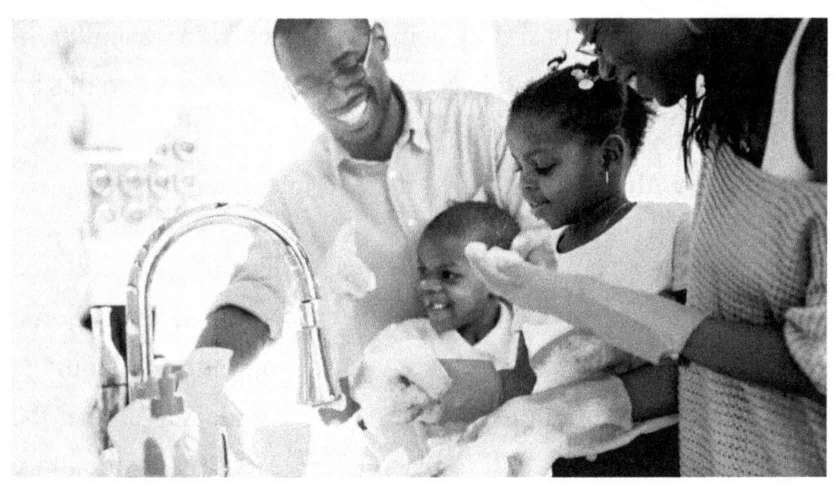

Teaching Respect and Responsibility

In the journey of parenting, there are few qualities as essential as respect and responsibility. As parents, we hold the key to instilling these virtues in our children, thereby guiding them toward becoming respectful and responsible individuals. We have to nurture these qualities from a young age, cultivating a foundation that will shape their character and interactions with the world around them.

Respect, the cornerstone of any healthy relationship, is something that children must learn from the very beginning. It is not enough for us to simply demand respect from our children; we must teach them what respect truly means. We can do this by modeling respectful behavior ourselves and treating our children and others with kindness, empathy, and understanding.

An important aspect of teaching respect is teaching our children to listen attentively. By actively listening to others, children learn to value different perspectives and opinions. Encourage them to listen without interrupting, to truly understand what the other person is saying before responding. This fosters a culture of respect and open communication within the family.

Respect also extends to the physical space we share. Teach your children to respect the belongings of others, whether it be toys, books, or personal space. By instilling a sense of responsibility for their actions, children learn to take care of their belongings and to respect the belongings of others.

Responsibility goes hand in hand with respect. It is the ability to take ownership of one's actions and the consequences that follow. Teaching responsibility begins with small tasks and gradually builds up to more significant responsibilities as children grow older. Encourage your children to take on age-appropriate chores and assignments, such as tidying their room or completing homework on time. This gives them a sense of accomplishment and teaches them the importance of fulfilling obligations.

One effective way to teach responsibility is through the establishment of routines. Children thrive on structure, and having a set routine instills a sense of order and accountability. Help your child create a daily routine that includes tasks such as making their bed, completing homework, and participating in household chores. By following the routine consistently, children learn the value of responsibility and develop a strong work ethic. It is important to remember that teaching respect and responsibility is an ongoing process. It requires patience, consistency, and understanding.

As parents, we must be mindful of our behavior and continually model the values we wish to instill in our children. By nurturing these qualities from an early age, we equip our children with the tools they need to navigate the world with respect and responsibility.

In conclusion, teaching respect and responsibility is an integral part of the parenting journey. By modeling respectful behavior, encouraging active listening, and fostering a sense of responsibility, we guide our children toward becoming respectful and responsible individuals.

Remember, this foundation will serve them well throughout their lives, enabling them to cultivate healthy relationships and make positive contributions to society.

CHAPTER 9

UNDERSTANDING YOUR CHILD'S EMOTIONS

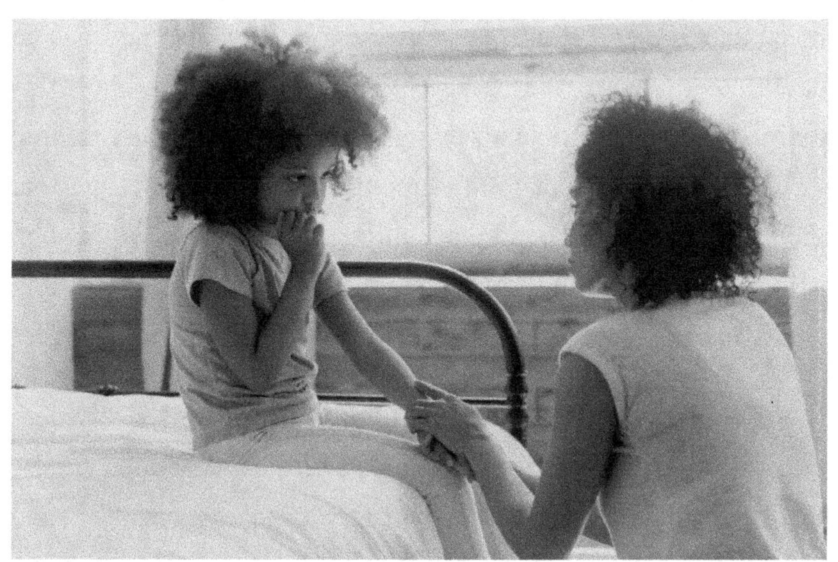

Understanding Your Child's Emotions

As parents, we strive to provide our children with a safe and nurturing environment where they can grow and thrive. We want them to be happy, but we also know that life is full of ups and downs. Emotions are an integral part of our human experience, and it is no different for our little ones. Understanding and helping our children navigate their emotions is crucial for their overall well-being.

Emotions can be complex, even for adults. For children, who are still learning to make sense of the world around them, understanding and expressing their emotions can sometimes be daunting. It is our role as parents to guide them through this journey, holding their hands every step of the way. The first step in understanding your child's emotions is to acknowledge that they are valid. Just like adults, children experience a wide range of emotions, including joy, sadness, anger, fear, and everything in between.

It is essential to create a safe and non-judgmental space where your child feels comfortable expressing their emotions freely. Pay attention to their body language, facial expressions, and verbal cues. Often, children may not have the words to articulate their feelings, but their nonverbal cues can provide valuable insights into their emotional state. By actively listening and observing, we can better understand what our children are experiencing.

Remember that emotions are not good or bad; they are simply a natural response to different situations. Teach your child that it is okay to feel angry, sad, or frustrated. By validating their emotions, you are sending a powerful message that their feelings matter and are worthy of acknowledgment. Help your child identify and label their emotions. Use age-appropriate language to describe different feelings. For example, you can say, "I can see that you are feeling upset right now" or "It looks like you're really excited about going to the park."

By giving emotions a name, you are helping your child develop emotional intelligence and the ability to communicate their feelings effectively. Encourage your child to express their emotions in a healthy way. Provide them with tools and strategies to cope with difficult emotions. These could include deep breathing exercises, drawing or painting, listening to calming music, or engaging in physical activities. By teaching them healthy coping mechanisms, you are equipping them with valuable skills that will serve them well throughout their lives.

Remember that your child is an individual with their own unique emotional experiences. Avoid comparing them to siblings or other children. Each child has their own emotional journey, and it is important to respect and honor their personal experiences.

Lastly, be a role model for your child. Show them how you manage your own emotions in a healthy way. Children learn by observing and imitating their parents' behavior. By demonstrating empathy, self-regulation, and healthy emotional expression, you are providing your child with a valuable blueprint for navigating their own emotions.

Understanding your child's emotions is an ongoing process that requires patience, empathy, and open communication. By creating a safe and supportive environment, you are empowering your child to embrace their emotions, learn from them, and grow into emotionally resilient individuals.

Remember, your child's emotional well-being is a precious gift, and you play a crucial role in nurturing it.

CHAPTER 10

FOSTERING POSITIVE THINKING

Fostering Positive Thinking

In this chapter, we will explore the power of positive thinking and how it can greatly impact our children's ability to have sweet dreams. Positive thinking is not just a fleeting thought or a temporary mindset; it is a way of life that can be cultivated and nurtured.

As parents, we have to be consistent; praying together as a family shows our children that we live as one unit. We play a crucial role in fostering positive thinking in our children. Our words, actions, and attitudes all have a profound impact on their perception of the world. By intentionally creating a positive environment, we can help our children develop a mindset that promotes happiness, resilience, and optimism.

As parents, we play a crucial role in fostering positive thinking in our children. Our words, actions, and attitudes all have a profound impact on their perception of the world. By intentionally creating a positive environment, we can help our children develop a mindset that promotes happiness, resilience, and optimism.

One essential aspect of fostering positive thinking is the language we use when communicating with our children. Our words have the power to shape their thoughts and beliefs.

Instead of dwelling on the negatives or focusing on what went wrong, we can choose to emphasize the positive aspects of any situation. For example, instead of saying, "You failed the test," we can reframe it by saying, "You gave it your best effort, and there's always room for improvement."

Another way to foster positive thinking is by encouraging our children to set realistic goals and celebrate their achievements, no matter how small. By doing so, we teach them that success comes in many forms and that every step forward is worth acknowledging. This mindset not only boosts their self-esteem but also instills a sense of gratitude and appreciation for their efforts.

Modeling positive thinking is equally important. Children are like sponges, absorbing everything around them. When they see us approaching challenges with a positive attitude, they learn to do the same. It is crucial to demonstrate resilience in the face of adversity, showing them that setbacks are temporary and can be overcome.

Creating a positive bedtime routine can significantly contribute to fostering positive thinking and sweet dreams. Before tucking them in, take a few moments to reflect on the day's positive experiences. Encourage your child to share what they are grateful for or something they enjoyed during the day. This practice helps shift their focus from any negative experiences, allowing them to go to bed with a positive mindset.

Moreover, incorporating positive affirmations into their nightly routine can be incredibly beneficial. Encourage your child to repeat affirming statements such as "I am capable," "I am loved," or "I am confident." By repeating these affirmations, they reinforce positive beliefs about themselves, which can have a lasting impact on their overall well-being.

Lastly, cultivating a positive thinking environment extends beyond bedtime. Encourage your child to engage in activities that bring them joy and promote positive thinking throughout the day. This could be anything from playing their favorite sport to engaging in creative arts or spending time with loved ones. By nurturing their passions and providing opportunities for positive experiences, we empower them to cultivate a positive mindset.

In conclusion, fostering positive thinking is a powerful tool that can greatly influence our children's ability to have sweet dreams. By using positive language, setting realistic goals, modeling positive thinking, and creating a positive bedtime routine, we can help our children develop the skills and mindset needed to approach life with optimism.

Remember, it is never too early to start fostering positive thinking in our little ones.

About the Author

Ursula Davis is a mother of 5 amazing children, and she has 10 beautiful grandchildren.

With over 30 years as a successful business owner in the beauty industry, she has appeared in top magazines around the world.

In addition, Ursula runs a nonprofit organization.

"A Guide to Good Parenting" is Ursula Davis' first published book.

Day	Breakfast	Lunch	Snacks	Dinner
MON	Set dosa + Ridge gourd peel chutney	Rice+ Ridge gourd dal+ Tindora fry	Fruits+ Mixed Nuts	Palak Paratha+ Dal
TUE	Palak Paratha+ Masala Curd	Cluster beans baath+ white bean veg salad	Fruits+ Mixed Nuts	Chapati+ Veg Sagu
WED	Set Dosa + Veg sagu	Quinoa Veg Khichdi+ Salad	Fruits+ Mixed Nuts	Paneer/Tofu Veggie Sandwich (brown bread)
THU	Paneer/Tofu Veggie Sandwich	Brown Rice Puliogare+ Moong sprouts veg salad	Fruits+ Mixed Nuts	Mixed Veg Pasta (white sauce)
FRI	Oats & Chia saffron porridge	Avocado Chickpeas Veg Salad+ roasted paneer/tofu	Fruits+ Mixed Nuts	Chapati+ Mangalore cucumber stir-fry

Must include in a day	*Veggies and Fruits for the week*
<ul><li>At least 3 veggies</li><li>2 or 3 fruits</li><li>Protein sources</li><li>Good fat</li><li>Yogurt or Buttermilk</li><li>Whole grains, at least thrice a week</li></ul>	<ul><li>Ridge gourd, Tindora</li><li>Spinach, Cluster Beans</li><li>Carrot, Beans, Peas</li><li>Capsicum, Broccoli</li><li>Mangalore Cucumber, Cucumber</li><li>Banana, Figs, Apple, Avocado</li></ul>

DAILY ROUTINE FOR KIDS

Morning

☐	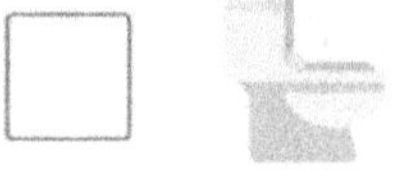	Go Potty
☐		Make Bed
☐	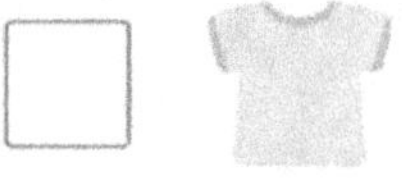	Get Dressed
☐		Brush Hair
☐	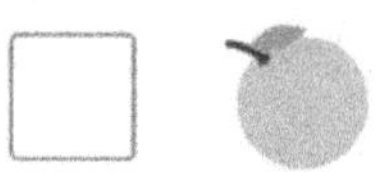	Eat Breakfast
☐	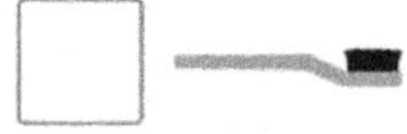	Brush Teeth
☐		School

Bedtime

☐	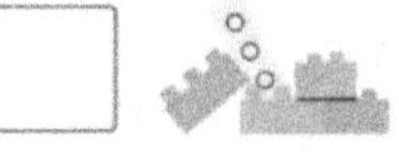	Clean up Toys
☐		Take Bath
☐		Pajamas
☐	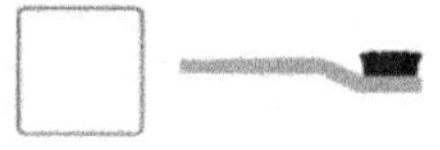	Brush Teeth
☐	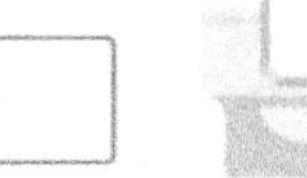	Go Potty
☐		Read a Book
☐	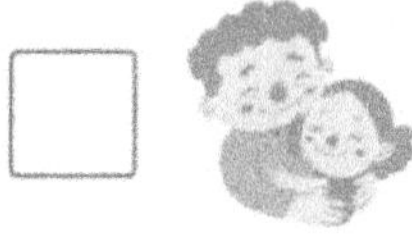	Hugs and Kisses

Daily Schedule

6:00-7:00 — Wake & Pray; toss in a load of laundry

7:00-7:30 — Kids wake, breakfast together

7:30-8:00 — Kids play; unload CLEAN dishes and load dirty dishes

8:00-9:00 — Get ready for the day, play together, switch laundry

9:00-11:00 — Outing

11:00-11:45 — Lunch Time

12:00-2:30 — Nap time & GO TIME for work

2:30-3:00 — Kids wake, Snack & Book Time

3:00-4:00 — Outdoor Play

4:00-5:00 — Independent Play, Dinner Prep

5:00-6:00 — Family Dinner Time

6:00-6:45 — Dinner Cleanup, load & start dishwasher

6:45-7:30 — Bathtime, books & bedtime for kids

7:30-8:00 — Fold clean laundry & put away

8:00-9:00 — Quality time with husband or power hour of work

Unwind, read & relax, go to bed

2 - 3 Years Old

- [ ] Make bed
- [ ] Take clothes to laundry room
- [ ] Put away laundry
- [ ] Pick up toys
- [ ] Dust furniture
- [ ] Feed pets
- [ ] Put clothes in dryer
- [ ] Match socks
- [ ] Clear place after meals

4 - 5 Years Old

- [ ] Set the table
- [ ] Clear the table
- [ ] Help cook dinner
- [ ] Carry and put away groceries
- [ ] Water plants
- [ ] Take sheets off bed
- [ ] Sort laundry
- [ ] Pull weeds
- [ ] Make a small snack
- [ ] Fold towels

6 - 9 Years Old

- [ ] Vacuum
- [ ] Fold laundry
- [ ] Put away laundry
- [ ] Sweep the floor
- [ ] Clean counters
- [ ] Empty dishwasher
- [ ] Help cook (wash produce, find ingredients, simple cutting)
- [ ] Get mail

10 - 15 Years Old

- [ ] Do laundry
- [ ] Mow the lawn
- [ ] Wash the car
- [ ] Cook a meal
- [ ] Wash dishes
- [ ] Clean the bathroom
- [ ] Take out trash
- [ ] Mop the floor